The Kiss of God

The Kiss of God

A Dialogue on Science, Mysticism, & Spiritual Practice

Father Thomas Keating
& Rabbi Zalman Schachter-Shalomi

C H A R I S

Contemplative Life,
Embodied Spirituality
& Sacred Activism

An Imprint of Albion-Andalus
Boulder, Colorado
2020

"The old shall be renewed,
and the new shall be made holy."
— Rabbi Avraham Yitzhak Kook

Albion-Andalus, Inc.
P. O. Box 19852
Boulder, CO 80308
www.albionandalus.com

Design and composition by Albion-Andalus
Cover design by D.A.M. Cool Graphics
Photos by Edis Jurcys 2005

Manufactured in the United States of America

ISBN-13: 978-1-7348750-0-3

For
Reb Zalman & Father Thomas.
Our Teachers

Preface

On May 25th, 2005, I brought my teacher, Rabbi Zalman Schachter-Shalomi, down to the Center for Contemplative Living in Denver, Colorado, to dialogue with Father Thomas Keating, who was then over from St. Benedict's Monastery in Snowmass, Colorado. It was the first time I had ever been in the presence of both of my two primary mentors in the spiritual life at the same time. I was far closer to Reb Zalman, traveling with him as his personal attendant and working with him on a number of books, but I had also been on the perifery of Father Thomas' circle of students for almost as long, and had had numerous significant encounters with him. Thus, I was thrilled to be bringing the two of them together, offering me the personal opportunity to learn with both of my mentors at once.

Just a few months earlier, filmmaker Cathy Zheutlin had approached me about how Reb Zalman might participate in a gathering of spiritual elders to be filmed for a proposed documentary to be called, *The Wisdom Keepers Project.* In the course of our conversations, she, representing the Wisdom Keepers Project, and I, representing the Reb Zalman Legacy Project, conceived of co-producing and bringing together Father Thomas and Reb Zalman to dialogue for a more modest documentary on science and spirituality.

The Kiss of God

Reb Zalman and I arrived at the Center for Contemplative Living in the morning, meeting our friend Rabbi Rami Shapiro who would introduce the film, the filmmaker Cathy Zheutlin, the videographer Edis Jurcys, Sister Bernadette Teasdale the directer of the center, as well as participants Joan Borysenko, Rabbi Steve Booth-Nadav, and Father Thomas. Among my favorite memories of that morning is the sight of Father Thomas trying on Reb Zalman's wide-brimmed black fedora as I walked into the room where they were talking, and a little later watching delightedly with Rami Shapiro as Reb Zalman extemporized a Hasidic melody on a nearby piano.

When all the cameras were set, we gathered for a period of meditation in the chapel, before settling in to watch the first session of dialogue between Reb Zalman and Father Thomas on science and the silence of God. When this session was complete, we broke for lunch, over which Reb Zalman pronounced the blessing. While still in the dining hall, Rabbi Rabbi Shapiro, Joan Borysenko, and Cathy Zheutlin asked both Father Thomas and Reb Zalman a series of questions about spiritual guidance and the spiritual path, before finally going outside to a nearby park for a second session of dialogue on the intimate "kiss of God."

From this last part of the dialogue, we took the title for the film, *The Kiss of God: A Dialogue of Devoutness between Father Thomas Keating and Rabbi Zalman Schachter-Shalomi*, released later that year. From the full transcripts of the original recordings (which contained more material than the edited documentary), I later edited a written version of the dialogue for *Spectrum: A Journal of Renewal Spirituality*, published as "The Kiss of God: A Dialogue on Science and Contemplative Spirituality" in Volume 3, Number 2, Summer-Fall, 2007. This was polished again for publication here, more than a decade later, through the Charis Foundation for New

Monasticism & InterSpirituality, which has roots in the teachings of both Rabbi Zalman Schachter-Shalomi and Father Thomas Keating.

— Netanel Miles-Yépez, Boulder, Colorado

July 1st, 2019

Part I

Dialogue in the Chapel

Rabbi Zalman Schachter-Shalomi: They want to know why we are here, why we are doing this. The simple answer is, because we love each other. There is a wonderful attraction I feel for you, and I feel from you to me, a mutual appreciation of how we are in the presence of God, and a recognition in each other of people who are in the 'service.' So I am glad you are here and that I am with you.

I remember meeting you and Father Basil Pennington many years ago, and I was very touched by the silence of Centering Prayer. Could you tell me, where does the issue of the "prayer of the heart" begin, as you do not exactly see that in the regular *missal?*

Father Thomas Keating: No, it presupposes some movement of trying to translate the text of the Bible, or the symbols of the liturgy into a kind of experiential touch or awakening of the Mystery that is present or communicated through those things. Some people like to throw them all out, but it is not a good idea to get rid of ritual altogether. To go through it and not around it leads you to the Mystery that is contained therein, and to which it points.

1

Reb Zalman: There is this wonderful statement in the Torah, "The people *saw* and they went backward; but Moses went into the dark fog, where God could be found." (Ex. 20:18)

Father Thomas: Yes . . . yes!

Reb Zalman: And that is where the Mystery is present. Often, in that kind of silence, in that way in which all the other voices are absent, as it says, "God is in the holy Temple, be silent before God all the earth." (Hab. 2:20)

Reb Zalman reading from a prayerbook in the chapel.

Father Thomas: Yes, most people are afraid of darkness, and now they leave the lights on all night in most cities. In the Bible, the darkness is not really 'darkness,' so much as an excess of light! You cannot see because it is too bright. Until your eyes can adjust, it feels like the deepest night; but it really is not dark.

Reb Zalman: Psalm 139.

Father Thomas: Which says?

Reb Zalman: "The darkness is not dark for you . . . darkness and light are the same to you." (Ps. 39:12)

Father Thomas: The Bible is so full of that image, like Moses' "cloud by night" (Ex. 40:38) and the caves as the symbol of desert and solitude.

Reb Zalman: Elijah coming to Mount Horeb. (1 Kings 19:8)

Father Thomas: Yes, you like that piece.

Reb Zalman: I like that a lot.

Father Thomas: And what do you get out of that?

Reb Zalman: Well, first of all, I am struck by the difference between the revelation to the people at Sinai—*boom, boom, boom*—lightning and thunder, and the manifestation comes. But Elijah goes as an individual, as a hermit, and God is not in the thunder, God is not in the storm, God is not in the earthquake. Then it says, there was a *kol d'mammah dakah*. The King James Bible translates it as "a still small voice." The Hebrew is better translated as "the subtle sound of stillness." (1 Kings 19:12)

Father Thomas: That is beautiful. I am very fond of that passage also. In one translation, it is called, "the sound of sheer silence." So what kind of a sound is that? It suggests that the divine presence is on a different frequency.

Reb Zalman: I like "sheer," 'transparent silence.'

It is interesting; right now, we are being recorded. If I were to whisper, they would have to amplify the sound of my voice. If it gets very quiet, almost silent, then the amplification has to be great even to hear a voice. So perhaps we need that great amplification of receptivity to hear a "voice" in the "sheer silence."

Father Thomas: I sometimes ask myself, why does it say that God passed by as "the sound of sheer silence"? And I sometimes I think, maybe because God went by so fast!

Reb Zalman: Ah-ha!

Father Thomas: God is very active, wouldn't you say?

Reb Zalman: Sometimes too fast for me!

Father Thomas: God is going by so fast, you could think God was not moving at all. We do not have the apparatus to reach God through the senses.

Reb Zalman: And we cannot comprehend God's time. If a thousand years are just a day, one second could be worlds without end!

Father Thomas: I love how scientists measure time around the Big Bang. They have counted-back to the first moment of anything, using the density of the material that eventually became the stuff of the whole universe, and the time that they figured is a trillionth of a trillionth of a trillionth of a second! How can you conceive or imagine a trillionth of second? It means nothing; our mind cannot wrap itself around that idea. It is a place where time disappears into eternity and becomes something beyond both.

Reb Zalman: Whenever the mind cannot grasp something, it is just baffled. The Mystery does not come until after the bafflement. So when you say, "a trillionth of a second," and you try to figure out what that is like, it is something like a can-opener for the mind, like a Zen *koan*.

Father Thomas: Exactly! A "can-opener" puts it very well.

It also works at the other end of the spectrum, where space gets bigger and bigger and farther and farther away, so that now they are saying that the galaxy is pushed aside by dark matter, and galaxies are going away so fast that in another few years, you will will not be able to see them anymore, and we will not have any idea what the first galaxies were like.

Reb Zalman: Yes, the speed of light will not be able to overcome the distance.

Father Thomas: The question I would like to have somebody in the scientific community answer for me is, what was 'there' before the galaxies arrived? Is 'nowhere' a place? And, if so, what is it like?

From that perspective, space disappears into spaciousness without limit. Time and space adjust themselves as being really a particular culture of our brain that sees reality from a rather limited perspective we call, the 'space-time continuum.'

Reb Zalman: We have a wonderful hymn that goes like this— *Adon olam, asher malakh, b'terem kol y'tzir nivra,* "You, sustainer of the world, were reigning before anything was created." That is to say, before the Big Bang is God's 'past.'

Then it says, *L'eyt na'asah b'hevtzo kol,* "after everything is finished," after the last black hole, "God will be Sovereign again." That is God's future. From the time of the Big Bang to the last black hole, that is God's present.[1] So you have a past before there is creation, a future after creation, and from the beginning of creation to the last black hole is God's present. Go figure that one!

But it is wonderful. When we stretch our mind this way, the mind cannot help but get out of the way and let the soul know. Then comes the big problem; how does the soul explain it to the mind? So you go with that for a while, you sink into it, going out of your human story and into a much bigger one.

Father Thomas: Nature is a marvelous revelation of God. The early Fathers of the Church used to say that God has given us two revelations: one, the "Book of Nature," which some might equate with science, and the book we call the Bible. So, in a manner of speaking, science and the Bible are equal in significance, because they both come from the same source; they can never really be in contradiction to each other. If there seems to be a contradiction, there is some lack of information, or a mind-set that does not take all of the aspects of reality into account.

Both reveal God equally, or God's plan for humanity. Of course, I am speaking of science that is genuine, not just an ideology, verifiable science in which the plan of God, especially in our time, is being revealed by extraordinary discoveries nearly every day! Both in the infinitesimal sub-atomic world of quantum mechanics, or the enormous infinite stretches of the galaxies at top speed on the way to nowhere!

Reb Zalman: When the Ezekiel speaks of various kinds of angels—*ofanim*, 'wheels,' *hayyot*, 'living beings,' and the *serafim*, the 'blazing ones'—I think of the orbiting planets as the *ofanim*, the 'wheels,' and the signs of the Zodiac as the *hayyot*, the 'living beings.' But those are still in *our* galaxy; farther away are the 'blazing ones,' the *serafim*, which are other galaxies. When you see the Horse-head Nebula, and the things we have seen through the Hubble telescope, it is so amazing! And the colors and energy that they represent!

But from another perspective, when we get into the revelation of Nature, we do not have to worry about commentary and dogma. It hits us very straight with every morning sunrise and at sunset.

7

I want to say this about the *Magisteria*—the traditional bodies of knowledge—in Judaism and Christianity; there is good teaching in each, but those teachings get wedded to time-bound cosmologies, and when they cannot be separated from these cosmologies, people like Giordano Bruno run into trouble. Saying that there is a greater cosmology than your current *Magisterium* is able to embrace becomes problematic. People get afraid. You find the same thing in Judaism today. If you were to say to some of the orthodox, "The world is older than 5765 years," they would get upset and begin to say illogical things trying to make this right, for instance, that God put 'false clues' into creation for us.

Reb Zalman and Father Thomas talking in the chapel.

Father Thomas: However they want to explain it, there cannot be any disagreement between genuine scientific discoveries and the Bible. It is a misconception of how to understand the Bible, as if it were a literal history like we write today.

Reb Zalman: And the third part of revelation that we do not often talk about is the one that happens in the soul. This is where I find that Centering Prayer and all forms of meditation are so important. They put you right back into the questions: what does your soul really know? And how do you explain it to the mind?

Father Thomas: Yes, that is always the problem.

There is a lot of research today about the heart, and they are saying that the heart 'thinks,' too; it is not just a pump!

Reb Zalman: And the skin! The skin is an extension of the brain, too. I think it is wonderful when you start to think about all the ways of sensing that are given to us, so that the *sensorium* serves consciousness. But when you reflect on how consciousness is conscious, that is where Buddhism has been of such help to us all, to Judaism and to Christianity, because it has a sense of reflecting on itself, the consciousness of itself. I think this is what puts us squarely in the presence of God, to know, how it is that I am conscious.

Father Thomas: Yes, there is the great God of Nature in these cosmic discoveries, the infinitesimal God who runs the sub-atomic world, with apparently great interest and effectiveness; but there is also a tenderness in God, the personal character of God, perhaps in all the world religions, but certainly a very significant part of Judaism and Christianity.

Reb Zalman: I do not want to dismiss the other ones either, because when I go into Hinduism, there is so much of that almost divine emotion toward people. But, of course, in Judaism, Christianity, and Islam, we speak very clearly about this, using words like, *Ya Raḥim, Ya Raḥman,* 'O Merciful, O Compassionate One!'

We were talking on another occasion about the Song of Song.

Father Thomas: I think that is an important revelation to put alongside both the Nature and biblical revelations of God.

Reb Zalman: That is where 'spousal mysticism' comes in; I think Mother Tessa Bielecki speaks well about this, that the soul and God have a spousal relationship. And you find that with Israel and God, and with the Church and her spouse. This spousal relationship, when it is present, feels like the acme of ecstasy; and when it is not there, there is such a longing for it, as it says in the Song of Songs, "On my bed at night, I sought him whom my soul loveth; I sought him and found him not." (3:1) And I think the issue of the longing of the soul has been discounted too much in organized religion. We feed people dogma too fast without letting them taste the hunger.

Part II
Dialogue in the Park

Reb Zalman: What do you think people mean when they say 'God'?

Father Thomas: It seems to me that when we say, 'God,' there is always a super-meaning involved, because it also means, 'not-God'—in the sense that any concept or idea that we can come up with is inadequate.

Reb Zalman: The word itself tells us that we do not know anything about God. And yet, at the same time, there is a feeling that says, 'How could this all happen?' People are now talking about 'intelligent design.' All of us who have been inolved in some form of contemplation and prayer feel that we did not make ourselves.

Father Thomas: The word 'God' usually refers to a concept of God that is presented by the culture, or by a particular religious community. By the process of spiritual growth, that idea is challenged, not to get rid of God, but to move beyond our *idea* of God.

Reb Zalman: That is right, beyond what you have conceived.

Father Thomas: The Ultimate Mystery, or Ultimate Reality, is perhaps a better term in a world of inter-penetrating cultures.

Father Thomas, Reb Zalman, and Rami Shapiro walking in the park.

Reb Zalman: We also have to encourage people to become iconoclasts, so that they take the childhood notions of God and destroy them. Without doing that, they cannot come to the Mystery.

Father Thomas: From the practical point of view, we need to find new symbols for young people, people living in the world, everyday lives, that enable them to feel God's presence—concrete symbols.

Reb Zalman: Right, "concrete" for the heart.

Father Thomas: For instance, thinking of creation in the 'womb of God,' because creation is not separate from God. I think this is the kind of image people are going to need today. Even science is talking in a kind of mystical language today, even more so than you might hear on a Sunday in church!

Reb Zalman: It is so interesting how science and mysticism can work together. For instance, I was so inspired by a person who was explaining the four letters of the divine name—*Y-H-V-H*—in terms of the four forces of the universe: electromagnetism, gravity, the strong nuclear force, and the weak nuclear force.

Father Thomas: The inter-connectedness of everything is what science is discovering, and that is the basic insight of the mystics. Physicists tell us that you cannot have a thought without effecting the whole universe, almost instantaneously.

Everything is one—one source. But we need to find the symbols that keep people in that perspective, where they are not overwhelmed by the diversity of God, the very realistic language of science. We need concrete symbols for people like me. This is why the idea of always being in the womb of God is so helpful.

Reb Zalman: It keeps us connected to the nurturing God.

Father Thomas: It brings out the divine feminine, too; patriarchal culture has been pretty stifling.

Reb Zalman: That is so true. You know, one of the nice things about going to the original languages is, in the Hebrew, the word, *Y-H-V-H*, the divine name, has an intrinsic sense of 'ever-present-ness,' and also of 'breath,' because they are all breath-letters. And then to speak of the Holy Spirit in Hebrew, it is a feminine word, *ru'ah ha'kodesh*, a 'she,' with that whole sense of the feminine sustaining. The "womb of God" is also wonderful because the Hebrew word for compassion is *rahamim,* and this is related to the word for 'womb.'

Father Thomas: Well, Isaiah hints at that when he says, "Can a woman forget the child of her womb? Even if she could, I will not forget you!" (Isaiah 49:15) which presumes that God must know what it is like to have a womb!

What do you think of this idea that we are born with two umbilical cords? One gets cut—that is the mother's, for the nourishment of the embryo—but the other is the spiritual nourishment received from God, and that is never cut, so one is never separated from God!

Reb Zalman: That is exactly how they explain it in Hasidism!

Part III
Dialogue on the Bench

Father Thomas: I like the story where Moses was being criticized by his 'staff.' You know, it happens to administrators all the time. So God said to Moses, "Bring them to the Tent of Meeting"—the place where Moses used to hang-out with God, to be refreshed by God—"and I'll straighten them out." (Num. 12:1-4) I am paraphrasing, of course. So Miriam and Aaron arrive, and God says, "You know, I have prophets all over the place; some I speak to in dreams, some have prophetic utterances about people's unconscious or their private lives; some I give prophecies for the future, but with my servant Moses, I speak mouth-to-mouth." (Num. 12:8)

A mouth-to-mouth encounter is a kiss!

Reb Zalman: You know, there is a beautiful description in the Midrash of how Moses died; it says that God kissed him. It is the same with the breath of Adam—God breathed into his nostrils the breath of life, and with a kiss he drew it out.

15

Father Thomas: This is the meaning of spirit—'breath'—and so the mouth of the soul is the spiritual well, according to the early Fathers of the Church. So you get the image in this mouth-to-mouth encounter of the opening one's spiritual well completely, in 360 degrees, to receive the pouring-in of the Holy Spirit.

Reb Zalman: And giving it back at the same time. For what does God get out of kissing us? It is like the question, 'If God has everything, then why does God have to create us?'

Father Thomas and Reb Zalman talking on the park bench.

Answer: because God is an atheist; God does not have a God. So what does it feel like for God to experience the love of God and the awe before God? For that, God needs human beings. And in the 'kiss,' God gets that love back. We get from God and God gets from us.

Father Thomas: One of the greatest gifts you can give God is to be willing to consent or receive this love and allow the spirit to be poured-in, unearned.

Reb Zalman: And also to give back with fervor! Not simply in passivity.

Father Thomas: True. It is a pouring into each other. It is an exchange of one's very being, a passionate kiss from the bottom of one's soul, not just one's heart.

Reb Zalman: And as Solomon says, it is "better than wine" (Song 1:2).

Father Thomas: Well that brings us to the Song of Songs, and its opening line, "Let him kiss me with the kisses of his mouth" (Song 1:2), which emphasizes the fact that there is more than one kind of kiss, and this aspect of God's erotic love for us has to be understood not as genital, but as a desire to communicate God's very being to us.

Reb Zalman: And also without having to be within the 'garments,' to be able to be totally open and vulnerable. Most people come to church or synagogue dressed-up in such a way that suggests that they do not want to be vulnerable. They bring their presentation of self—'This is who I am; this is what I do in the world.'

Father Thomas: Yes, not quite what it is all about.

Reb Zalman: And so, spiritual 'nakedness' is necessary for getting into that connection of the 'kiss.'

Father Thomas: It suggests the humility of God. God wants to give the divine self away, not to take possession of anyone. God does not need any possessions.

Reb Zalman: Right! That is why I think that Judaism and Christianity could talk about a *tantra* that would be very, very special.

Father Thomas: Yes, we should emphasize that incredible love of God that seems to want to throw itself away, that even wishes not to be God.

Reb Zalman: That is what we call *tzimtzum* in the Kabbalah, the self-limitation of God.

Father Thomas: God cannot die, so the next best thing is to make us equal to God.

Reb Zalman: So *kenosis* is what they are talking about, how God 'pours' the divine self into us. So God has decided to be 'Tom Keating' and 'Zalman Schachter' today and is having a lot of fun!

Father Thomas: The lowest form of intellectual beings!

The tenderness of God, the nurturing motherliness, the care, protection, closeness—these are the things we need symbols of for our people immersed in the world outside, where there is little to remind them of God.

Reb Zalman: That is why so much more happens around the table. You know, the Last Supper was not a situation where Jesus took them to the Temple; they were just hanging around the table.

Father Thomas: Yes!

Reb Zalman: The wedding at Cana is the same kind of situation. And so much with the Hasidic masters happens not at the synagogue, but at the table. We call it the rebbe's *tish*.

Father Thomas: Well, in that Palestinian culture, meals were much more meaningful; they signified identification with the people that you sat at the table with.

Reb Zalman: Just breaking bread was a symbol of making peace, and making a covenant.

Father Thomas: Companionship, from the Latin, *com*, 'with,' and *pan*, 'bread'! Eating bread together is to share their being, their values, their needs, their sufferings—everything. So for God to share a meal with us is to create identification.

Reb Zalman: And the inter-generational connection also happens around the table. Grandpa telling a story to the kids, and while they are eating, they are imbibing the tale together with the food, interiorizing all of it. I wish people would bring more holiness to the table.

Father Thomas: The problem is that they do not even stay at the table; they go out to a restaurant.

Reb Zalman: Or see it as a time for entertainment.

Reb Zalman: I like the story that Tolstoy tells of the three times that Jesus came to sup' with the shoemaker; do you remember that story?

Father Thomas: Vaguely—remind me.

Reb Zalman: He has a dream, and Jesus says, "I'm going to come and sup' with you." So he prepared breakfast and had it all waiting when an old man comes the door who is hungry. He looks at the old man and decides to feed him the breakfast. Then he prepares a lunch, and some children come who are hungry. Then he prepares supper, and a woman comes and eats up the supper. Finally, he gets to the place where he falls asleep again, and says in his dream, "O Lord, why did you not come? I prepared for you three times." And Jesus responds, "What do you mean? I came three times!"

That is a wonderful, "Whatever you have done to the least of my children" (Matt. 25:40) story. These stories warm the heart.

Father Thomas: I was thinking of an image that struck me, and I have shared this with a lot of people. How did you feel when you held your first grandchild? Actually, if you were grandma and had been through birthing and now you are just enjoying the net result without having to go through all the pain, this little treasure is just a sheer bundle of joy. Now suppose the baby opens its eyes and smiles, and poor grandma goes into an ecstasy for three days!

Father Thomas and Reb Zalman exchanging blessings.

Part IV
Question and Answer Session

Joan Borysenko: Since we are about to start a school for interspiritual mentors, helping people find spiritual direction, my question is this: in each of your traditions, what is 'spiritual guidance'?

Father Thomas: Spiritual guidance can be good, bad, or indifferent. It requires experience and training. It is the 'spiritual companioning,' in the sense of walking with someone in their spiritual journey, listening together to what the Spirit—who is the true guide, at least in the Christian tradition—is trying to say to this person through their own intuition. So it is not so much a question of telling them what to do, or giving them some particular books to read— although this could happen from time-to-time, depending on what the discernment is—but it is the discerning itself, the listening.

I think discernment is related to listening to what God is trying to communicate by way of general or particular guidance to the directee. So that is more of a spiritual companionship, or 'soul-friending,' as they sometimes call it, today— beaming back to somebody what they really feel called to do themselves, and supporting them in their resolutions, or at least in their insights.

Reb Zalman: It is really necessary to be with a person and to see what issues from them; and yet, there is also an element that has to do with a practical 'know-how,' because there is always a difference between my 'is' and my 'ought.' People are often aware of their 'ought,' but do not know how to move from 'ought' to 'is.' So what is needed is what they call in Buddhism, *upaya*, 'skillful means'—and all of the traditions have skillful means, as we see in someone like Brother Lawrence in Christianity, or Reb Elimelekh of Lizhensk in Judaism—and when one begins to act on these 'skillful means,' the transformational aspect of them begins to work on the individual.

Also, as you mentioned, discernment is also necessary, to know exactly what is true, and to be able to tell it apart from what masquerades as divine. This is necessary, because people often have a sense of grandiosity about themselves, and have not actually taken care of what they need to take care of on the spiritual path. I remember one man expressed this situation in terms of putting "whipped-cream on top of garbage." Very often, the spiritual—when it has not taken care of some of the basic *metanoia*, that shift in being and behavior—leads to an unhelpful grandiosity.

I once heard something from a Christian sister that really touched me; she said, "All of spiritual direction deals with one thing— reducing one's resistance to God."

Father Thomas: Very good. Very good.

Cathy Zheutlin: Is there one experience that really turned you around?

Reb Zalman: Well, it is very much like fishing. At one point you get 'hooked,' and you want to run away, not wanting to be caught, but God has a way of reeling-you-in slowly, giving you some space so you do not break the line, the connection, but giving you some space to fight it. If I were to look at just how much fighting was going-on inside of me in the early days, and how much I had to learn . . . There was one point at which Rev. Howard Thurman asked me this question, "Don't you trust the Holy Spirit?" Actually, he said it in Hebrew, *ru'ah ha'kodesh.*

Can you imagine an African-American teacher in the 1950s saying to a Jew in Hebrew, "Don't you trust the *ru'ah ha'kodesh?*" Well, it shook me very, very strongly. But then, what are you going to reply, 'No?' Who else are you going to trust? So it takes a very deep engagement, and each time, the line pulls you in a little bit more and more, until finally, there comes the net that catches you. That is how I feel the process goes.

Father Thomas: There is a sermon by Meister Eckhardt called, "Hooked by Divine Love." The idea is that once you swallow the hook, you can never get away; no matter how hard you swim in the opposite direction, you are a 'gonner.' It is just a matter of time. The divine fisher keeps 'reeling-you-in,' as you said, until you have to surrender.

But, with regard to spiritual guidance, as you say, there is a lot of basic material that you need to know. However, a lot of the basics are available now in books; it is not as if we were in a pre-Gutenberg Bible era, where a spiritual guide would have to give you the whole tradition. The fundamentals are available. It seems to me as if the emphasis has moved toward listening, deep listening to what the Spirit is saying to this particular person.

Joan Borysenko, Father Thomas, Reb Zalman, and Rami Shapiro.

Reb Zalman: Well, I want to go beyond the books, first. I remember a time I was sitting with your colleague, Father Basil Pennington, doing a *Vipassana* practice, which was not quite a "prayer of the heart" for me, so I tuned-into the vibration of what he was doing, and I was then able to do it myself as a "prayer of the heart." So my sense is that, besides the books, you have to have a mentor who is 'tuned-in.' When that attunement happens, everything in the book starts to make sense. And without the attunement, the book does not help very much.

Father Thomas: Very, very true.

At the same time, if the spiritual guide does not have that particular *charis*, or inner experience, then you can sit as much as you like with them, and nothing is going to happen from that source. So, that is why everything really depends not just on training—lots of people can get a degree—but on the experience of a practice that one has interiorized over years and years, so that you really know how to listen, and are willing to hear what the true Guide is trying to say, or more particularly, what the Spirit is saying.

Mary Mrozowski told me how she once sat and listened in silence for a long time to someone, and in the end, they get up and left without her ever saying a thing. Later the person said to her, "Oh, you helped me so much, Mary; I can't thank you enough." What helped them was that she was totally herself, and that she was there with the whole of her being, just listening, and that was a kind of a sounding board that reflected back to them.

Reb Zalman: Being present with the heart made the difference.

Father Thomas: And that is a great gift that does not come with a degree.

Rabbi Rami Shapiro: To what extent is 'listening' a core metaphor for spiritual practice?

Father Thomas: It is definitely a core metaphor. It is not the only one, but at a certain level, all of the core symbols or words tend to merge into one, just as 'deep listening' is really 'silence.' I notice that in the Hebrew Bible, whenever God has anything to say, it always starts out with "Hear O Israel," and this is not an invitation just to listen with the ears; God wants us to have people listen with the heart; as with the mouth-to-mouth exchange, the ultimate listening is total receptivity, a welcoming attitude.

Reb Zalman: In Yiddish, we have the word *hehren*, which means 'to hear,' and *der hehren*, which means 'to realize.'

But I want to say something else about all this spiritual stuff. Sometimes people come and they tell me about what they do in meditation, and I feel that they are putting themselves into a kind of bubble, separating from everything around them, but not necessarily doing this in the presence of God.

Father Thomas: Yes.

Reb Zalman: That sense that, in my awareness, I am transparent to God; this is also important. If I do not see myself in the view of God, then whatever I am going to do is still going to be ego-enhancing, and not that which has to do with Spirit. So you might say that there is 'hearing,' and there is 'being seen.' And in Hebrew, the words for 'being seen' and having 'fear of God' ("which is the beginning of wisdom" – Prov. 9:10) are related. When I suddenly become aware that I am being seen, there is a startle reflex—all of a sudden I realize I am not alone.

Father Thomas: There is one other aspect of listening that is important here, and it is suggested in St. John of the Cross' description of contemplation, in which he says, "Contemplation is total receptivity." Well, in listening, what are you doing? Nothing. You are totally attentive, so that you do not miss a word or a note of the 'music.' It is to be totally present and open. So openness seems to be another keyword for contemplation; it why we called my book, *Open Mind, Open Heart.*

There is this distinction in the Spanish of St. John of the Cross' writing—'total receptivity' doesn't mean 'passivity.' It means an attitude of welcoming receptivity, which is quite different. It is like a little bird in the spring waiting to get the worm from mother; the bird is practically fifty percent beak with its mouth so wide open. It is the opening of the spiritual will, a mouth of the soul that can receive the whole of the message, which is the gift of the divine nature itself. To be hungry for that experience is to listen at the deepest levels. 'Hunger,' 'longing,' 'darkness,' 'desert,' 'solitude'—these words are just different facets of the same reality.

In the story of the transfiguration of Christ, there are about twelve keywords which point to the different aspects of this reality. They go up a mountain—*solitude.* There is a *dark cloud,* which resonates with Moses and the Israelites trip through the desert to Mount Sinai. There is the *Voice,* so they were *listening.* And then there is the message out of the cloud, "This is my beloved son, *listen* to him." (Luke 9:35) So deep listening is it.

Reb Zalman: We were talking before about the issue of the 'kiss.' I can also imagine a person being so passive that they do not respond to the kiss. That would be the wrong way to

29

do it. When you are saying that you are kissing back, as it were, that is also one of those ways of talking about *listening*.

Father Thomas: Very true. Though I do not think there is much danger in a kiss from God; there is no chance of not responding to that!

Reb Zalman: No. But if we go to Jean de Caussade, we do see that sometimes people get to be so quietistic that they do not respond. And when you look at the word, 'listening,' it is connected with the word, 'obeying.' "Speak for thy servant listens" (1 Sam. 3:10) has to do with the notion that I will listen to your command; I will do it. It is willingness not only to receive what comes, but to act on that command.

Father Thomas: I can see that this is your preoccupation with this issue of listening, and some of the other issues, too; you want to make sure there is some response. That is why in the Centering Prayer practice we do not only recommend having an 'intention' of being open to God, but a 'consent,' which is to put it into practice by appropriately sitting there and directing one's attention to the divine presence. As John Calvin used to say, "Hell is paved with good intentions." I do not exactly agree with that saying, but we need more than a mere 'intention.'

To listen to the word of God is to resonate with the creative word of God, the creative energy that said, "Let there be light" (Gen. 1:3), let there be life, let there be love. So *lectio divina*—divine reading—is actually prayerful listening, not just reading, listening to the book or the text that we believe is inspired by God or the Holy Spirit. It is not like reading the newspaper.

Reb Zalman: There is something not fully done when I just read the text. There is something about giving 'consent,' as you mentioned before, that is really important. I say, 'It really is so.' If I can say, 'It really is so,' it makes all the difference. I call that the issue of so-beingness—*aseity*—'that is how it is.' Once I make up my mind that 'that is how it is,' it takes on a whole other reality and enters into my reality-map

Blessings

Reb Zalman: There is this wonderful sentence that says, "Still in old age, they will be as juicy in the courts of the Lord as a palm tree, or like a cedar in Lebanon." (Ps. 92:12-14) May this be our blessing that we will yet see good to happen in the world, that the concerns that we have at this time will be addressed, and that God will send a blessing for good government and bring us closer to our messianic age.

Father Thomas: Yes. And may the spirit of God pour love into your heart and mind and spirit, to fill you with the wisdom to bring love to the elders, as you are doing in your wonderful ministry for the aging, and to continue to inspire young rabbis with the mystical tradition of Judaism. And may God grant you many more years, and the ultimate transformation into perfect love.

Reb Zalman: Amen!

Contemplative Life,
Embodied Spirituality
& Sacred Activism

Charis Foundation for New Monasticism & InterSpirituality
is dedicated to the emergence of a newly conceived
contemplative life that embraces the ideals of all of the world's
wisdom traditions. Charis Foundation strives to support the
development of an interspiritually-based new monasticism
through a series of dialogue-based retreats for current and
future spiritual leaders, written and audio-visual resources
for new monastic life, the preservation of teachings from
interspiritual pioneers, and partnerships with monasteries
and other contemplative centers to provide a place of retreat
and training for new monastics. Through these activities,
Charis Foundation wishes to support new monastic and
interspiritual seekers of all types in their desire to commit to
a disciplined contemplative life, while remaining connected
to the world and its needs, especially as related to social
justice and environmental responsibility.

Printed in Great Britain
by Amazon

29465082R00024